HAL•LEONARD
INSTRUMENTAL PLAY-ALONG

AUDIO ACCESS INCLUDED

PLAYBACK+
Speed • Pitch • Balance • Loop

TROMBONE

Movie and TV Music

Audio Arrangements by Peter Deneff

To access audio visit:
www.halleonard.com/mylibrary

Enter Code
2490-1476-5934-6656

ISBN 978-1-5400-2068-0

Visit Hal Leonard Online at
www.halleonard.com

Contact Us:
Hal Leonard
7777 West Bluemound Road
Milwaukee, WI 53213
Email: info@halleonard.com

In Europe contact:
Hal Leonard Europe Limited
Distribution Centre, Newmarket Road
Bury St Edmunds, Suffolk, IP33 3YB
Email: info@halleonardeurope.com

In Australia contact:
Hal Leonard Australia Pty. Ltd.
4 Lentara Court
Cheltenham, Victoria, 3192 Australia
Email: info@halleonard.com.au

THE AVENGERS
from THE AVENGERS

TROMBONE

Composed by
ALAN SILVESTRI

CAPTAIN AMERICA MARCH

from CAPTAIN AMERICA

TROMBONE

By ALAN SILVESTRI

DOCTOR WHO XI

TROMBONE

By MURRAY GOLD

DOWNTON ABBEY

(Theme)

TROMBONE

Music by JOHN LUNN

GAME OF THRONES

Theme from the HBO Series GAME OF THRONES

TROMBONE

By RAMIN DJAWADI

GUARDIANS OF THE GALAXY

from GUARDIANS OF THE GALAXY

TROMBONE

Composed by TYLER BATES,
DIETER HARTMANN, TIMOTHY WILLIAMS
and KURT OLDMAN

HAWAII FIVE-O THEME

from the Television Series

TROMBONE

By MORT STEVENS

MARRIED LIFE
from UP

TROMBONE

By MICHAEL GIACCHINO

OUTLANDER THEME
(The Skye Boat Song)

TROMBONE

Traditional Music
Arranged by BEAR McCREARY

PROLOGUE AND PROLOGUE PART 2

from BEAUTY AND THE BEAST

TROMBONE

PROLOGUE
Music by ALAN MENKEN

PROLOGUE PART 2
Music by ALAN MENKEN and CHRISTOPHER BENSTEAD

REY'S THEME
from STAR WARS: THE FORCE AWAKENS

TROMBONE

Music by JOHN WILLIAMS

Broadly

Tempo I

THEME FROM THE X-FILES

from the Twentieth Century Fox Television Series THE X-FILES

TROMBONE

By MARK SNOW

TEST DRIVE

from the Motion Picture HOW TO TRAIN YOUR DRAGON

TROMBONE

By JOHN POWELL